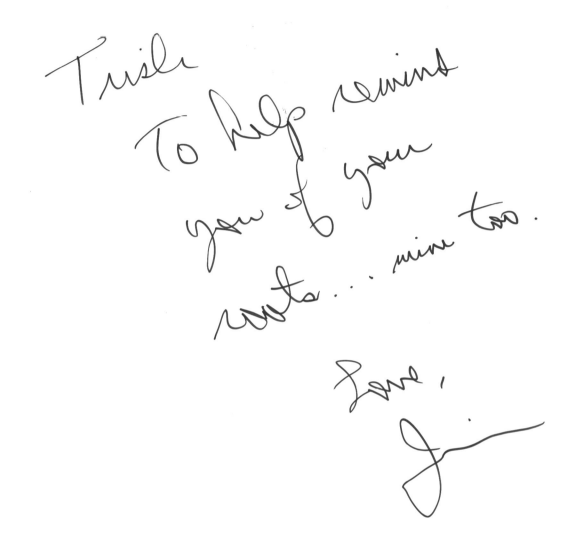

Trish

To help remind
you of your
roots . . . mine too.

Love,
J

B A R N S

CAROL M. HIGHSMITH AND TED LANDPHAIR

CRESCENT BOOKS

NEW YORK

FRONT COVER:
The 1888 Kleffner
Ranch barn in East
Helena, Montana, has
three floors and
seventy windows.
BACK COVER:
George Washington
built a sixteen-sided
treading barn on his
Mount Vernon estate
in Virginia. Above, a
barn with painted silo
near Sycamore,
Illinois, and a classic
barn near Forbidden
Caverns in Sevier
County, Tennessee.
PAGE 1: A western
hay barn peeks over a
hill on California's
Central Coast. PAGES
2–3: Shelburne
Farms' five-story barn
in Vermont once
housed eighty teams
of horses.

This 2000 edition is published by
Crescent Books®, an imprint of
Random House Value Publishing, Inc.,
201 East 50th Street, New York, N.Y. 10022.

Crescent Books® and colophon
are registered trademarks of
Random House Value Publishing, Inc.

Random House
New York • Toronto • London • Sydney • Auckland
http://www.randomhouse.com/

Printed and bound in China

Library of Congress Cataloging-in-Publication Data
Highsmith, Carol M., 1946–
Barns / Carol M. Highsmith and Ted Landphair.
p. cm.
ISBN 0-517-20875-X
1. Barns—United States Pictorial works.
I. Landphair, Ted, 1942– . II. Title.
NA8230.H54 2000   99-37452
728.922'0973022—dc21   CIP

8 7 6 5 4 3 2 1

Project Editor: Donna Lee Lurker
Designed by Robert L. Wiser, Archetype Press, Inc.,
Washington, D.C.

*The authors extend special appreciation to
Charles A. Leik, editor of the on-line* Barn
Journal, *for sharing his expertise on barns and
their historic importance to the nation.* Barn
Journal, *at http://museum.cl.msu.edu/barn/, is
an outstanding resource on historic barns, barn
construction and restoration, and barn lore.*

*We also wish to thank the following for their
generous assistance and hospitality in
connection with the completion of this book:*

Alex Johnson Hotel
Rapid City, South Dakota

Colony Inn Restaurant
Amana, Iowa

Corner House Bed and Breakfast
West Amana, Iowa

Country Suites
Bismarck, North Dakota

Historic Charleston Bed and Breakfast
Charleston, West Virginia

Holiday Inn
Amarillo, Texas

Holiday Inn Select at the Pyramids
Indianapolis, Indiana

Josephine Bed & Breakfast
Billings, Montana

Hotel Phillips
Bartlesville, Oklahoma

Radisson Reed House Hotel and Suites
Chattanooga, Tennessee

Ramada Inn Copper King
Butte, Montana

Silvermine Tavern Inn and Restaurant
Norwalk, Connecticut

Susan Albrechts,
Montana State Department of Travel

Lynne Liscek Black, Coastal Fairfield County,
Connecticut, Convention and Visitor Bureau

Zoe and Joe Gillespie, Lexington, Kentucky

Wayne Glass, Bethesda, Maryland

Cindy Harrington,
West Virginia Tourist Commission

Robin Hennes, Amana Colonies, Iowa,
Convention & Visitors Bureau

Pat Hertz, North Dakota Tourism

Landon Howard, Chattanooga, Tennessee,
Area Convention & Visitors Bureau

Carrie Kenney, Butte, Montana,
Convention & Visitors Bureau

Ruth McKinney, Rockford, Illinois

Robert W. McQuown, Mantua, Ohio

Eric Miller, Amarillo, Texas,
Convention & Visitor Council

Holly Raver, The Indianapolis Project,
Indianapolis, Indiana

Mary Stadick Smith,
South Dakota Department of Tourism

Tina Smith, Bartlesville, Oklahoma,
Visitors Bureau

FOREWORD

In a bygone era, when the nation lived closer to the land, the first thing a farmer built after he bought a new spread was not a farmhouse but a barn. He and his neighbors would gather on a piece of high ground to raise a sturdy, all-in-one structure to shelter his livestock, store his grain, and protect his wagon. As the number of family farms dwindles before the onslaught of consolidation and suburban sprawl, many barns that survive have become nostalgic landmarks.

Early barns often reflect the heritage of their builders. Dutch barns with gable roofs—often with a cupola for ventilation—became the American classic. Norwegians and Swedes built "bank barns" with a lower entrance and a long earthen ramp that enabled wagons to drive directly into the upper level. Scots-Irish farmers erected crib barns with several pig or cattle stalls and covered them with tin or asphalt roofs. Western farmers with large cattle herds topped their barns with high peaked or gambrel roofs—shaped a bit like a horse's hind leg—that greatly increased the capacity of the haymows and often with a pentice overhang with a pulley to hoist hay bales into a loft. Czechs and Russians built combination house-barns. Cedar shingles and bay windows— for ventilation—were common New England adornments. Farmers like George Washington discovered the advantages of a round barn or round-appearing structure with twelve to sixteen sides. It was roomier than a rectangular barn, needed few interior supports, and was remarkably resistant to even tornadic winds.

Massive and relatively unadorned barns had simple elements of decoration. Chief among them was their color—usually red because it was the cheapest pigment. Grandiose advertisements for chewing tobacco, patent medicine, waterfalls, and rock formations emblazoned thousands of barns. The farmer got his barn freshly painted in the bargain. "Hex signs," weather vanes, and lightning rods were other decorative touches. Barns became the perfect "canvas" for oversized portraits, animal likenesses, and fanciful designs. Of course, aficionados would argue that barns themselves are works of art.

Thousands of barns were left to rot as farmers turned to sturdier, climate-controlled metal sheds that could hold large machinery. When small farms were combined, fewer barns were needed. Many farmers also lacked the capital or insurance to rebuild barns that burned or blew down.

An incredible array of historical societies, professional and amateur architects, Internet web sites, collectors' groups, and barn lovers have rescued old barns. The National Trust for Historic Preservation not only helped save hundreds of barns through its "Barn Again!" program, it even staged an old-fashioned barn raising *inside* the National Building Museum in Washington. Thousands of barns have been restored, not for agriculture but as historic museums, antique shops, real estate offices, firehouses, and bed-and-breakfast inns. These are valued relics but they lose historic character apart from a cornfield or pasture.

Barns that survive on the farm or live in our memories are cherished harvest homes. We stop to admire a beautifully preserved one, to pause over a yellowed photograph, to wonder at the hard but honorable work that went on inside a forlorn and sagging ruin, and to sigh at the erosion of an American tradition that the passing of barn after barn represents.

OVERLEAF: Like many barns in Maine, this shingle barn at Grandview Farm near Dover is attached to the farmhouse, facilitating easy access in the frigid winter months. Typical of a New England barn, the entry doors are at the end. Numerous small windows give dairy cows—not to mention a farmer who milks them— plenty of light.

The gambrel roof at this barn (above) in Little-
ton, New Hampshire, greatly increases the
volume of an upper-story hayloft. "Gambrel"
is a French word, roughly meaning "meat hook,"
and reflects the roof's abrupt change in pitch.
Laudholm Farms (right) in Wells, Maine,
became a much-studied model farm, on which
George C. Lord, president of the Boston and
Maine Railroad, and his descendants exhibited
canning, milking, and mowing techniques—
and even gathered seaweed as fertilizer.

Block Island, Rhode Island, boasts Victorian hotels, stone walls, and quaint barns like Adrian Mitchell's (opposite). Barns like the stone masterpiece (top left) at Hancock Shaker Village near Pittsfield, Massachusetts, and the red beauty (bottom left) near Barnet, Vermont, were built years before round barns became popular in the Midwest. Impressionist J. Alden Weir kept a working farm (overleaf) surrounding his art studio in Ridgefield, Connecticut. The farm is now a National Historic site.

Actress Joanne Woodward (top right) dedicated the carriage barn that was reassembled, cobblestone by stone, at the Museum of Westport History in Connecticut. Her husband, Paul Newman, contributed much of the restoration funds. Brad and Chris Parliman's barn (bottom right) in Coventry, Connecticut, overlooks the old post road between Philadelphia and Boston. Bayberry Farm (opposite) near East Haddam, Connecticut, features a livestock barn and a hay barn made of chestnut wood in the mid-nineteenth century.

Residents of a gated community in Greenwich, Connecticut, enjoy gardens and beaches on the once-private estate where this barn and toolshed (above) stands. Behind the 1725 "Miss Amelia's Cottage" in East Hampton on New York's Long Island stand two carriage houses (left). The one to the right is now a carriage museum, reflecting the era when buggies were made in the area. A concrete milkhouse for straining and storage abuts the elegantly decorated, louvered barn (overleaf) in Duncannon, Pennsylvania.

Now abandoned, this dairy farm (above) near Carlisle, Pennsylvania, was once a thriving operation. The huge silos stored ensilage—green fodder such as chopped hay, alfalfa, clover, or shredded corn—that compacts tightly, keeping out air and preventing spoilage. The old dairy barn (right) near Waynesboro, Pennsylvania, features a forebay, or overhang. A cantilevered upper haymow, resting on joists, extends several feet over the basement level. This style of barn has been traced to the early cantons of Switzerland.

The crop has been harvested outside this huge Pennsylvania barn (above) near Shady Grove. This is a "bank barn." On this side, the barn is entered directly at the upper level. The terrain falls sharply on the other side, and entry is at a lower level. Roof ventilators, which pull moisture and heat from the building, are both practical and decorative. Spring weeds bathe a utilitarian block barn (opposite), with its galvanized steel roof, in color near Gapland, Maryland.

A huge barn (opposite) near Mechanicsville, Maryland, is the centerpiece of a fruit farm. Like many barns today, this structure is unadorned. Farmers once typically took pains to highlight their barns with contrasting trims and door designs, but practicality and the pressures of time intervened and diminished the practice. Choking vines have overtaken this abandoned and unpainted Maryland barn (above). Vandals, arsonists, and Mother Nature have delivered the *coup de grâce* to many such barns.

Although Central Pennsylvania is the nation's best-known Amish region, Amish farmers in several states maintain trim spreads recognizable by the absence of electric power lines. A tidy Amish structure with high eaves (above) is in Saint Mary's County, Maryland. This stylized stable (opposite) with horizontal siding is near Marshall in western Virginia's "horse country." The impressive barn (overleaf) near Shenandoah National Park in Virginia has such a deep forebay that posts were needed to support it.

A cantilevered barn (opposite) near the Eagle's Nest Airport in Waynes-boro, Virginia, casts a lovely reflection in an adjacent pond. By opening the sliding doors above ground level, a farmer could throw out straw after hay thrashing. Not far away, suburbia encroaches on an old hay barn (above). Here a practical farmer, instead of adding a shed to his barn, put a shallow roof over a shelter in which manure can easily be removed by tractor.

In upland Appalachia, farms tend to be less pros-
perous and barns smaller and less sturdily con-
structed than elsewhere. Many barns were never
painted. Farms like this spread (left) near Bas-
tian, Virginia, emphasize grazing rather than the
production of grain. In tobacco barns like this
one (above) in Watauga County, North Carolina,
blended varieties are air cured. Other types
of tobacco are cured in sealed barns into which
heat is introduced through a system of flues.

To feed livestock today, many farmers simply roll hay in bales of twelve hundred pounds or more. Like a thatched roof, the rolls shed most water rather than absorbing it. This spread (opposite) lies along old North Carolina Highway 86 outside Hillsborough. The owner of this farm (above) in the Maggie Valley of North Carolina, near Smoky Mountain National Park, found a beautiful and flat, if sometimes stormy, spot between the mountains.

An East Tennessee barn (top right) promotes its owner's collectibles business. Many classic mid-South barns were adorned with advertisements for Mail Pouch chewing tobacco and attractions like Ruby Falls and Rock City (bottom right). In return, farmers got their barns painted for free. One barn (opposite) at the Cobblestone Farm in Ann Arbor, Michigan, is narrow with high eaves. A gem among polyhedron, or multi-sided, barns is the nine-sided Door Prairie Barn (overleaf) in I a Porte, Indiana.

Sunset casts a glow over an impressive dairy barn (above) with three traditional silos and a smaller steel silo near Bruce in northern Wisconsin. Valuable shelled corn goes in the steel silo, which greatly retards spoilage. Cliff Keepers found that a relative's barn near Gilman, Wisconsin, made a terrific easel (right) on which to celebrate a Super Bowl victory by the state's beloved Green Bay Packers. Earlier, the lady with the winsome smile sported a Wisconsin Badgers' T-shirt.

Still more silos punctuate the landscape of a farm (opposite) near Leland, Wisconsin. Prominent is a modern, high-volume pole barn supported by creosoted poles. There were once hundreds of round wood or stone barns like the forlorn example (above) near children's book author Laura Ingalls Wilder's childhood home in Pepin, Wisconsin. Intricate framing (overleaf) helps connect the hayloft of the Joshua Secrest Octagonal Barn in Johnson County, Iowa, with an adjacent cattle feeding shed.

Luther College in Decorah, Iowa, now cares for this big red barn (left) that was once a working farm museum. Nearby, the college is replicating the wild prairie that pioneers encountered on their way west. Iowa's Amana Colonies—once a German-speaking collective society—feature several "pass through" barns like this one (above) right in the seven little villages that make up the colonies. Two roof styles are visible on barns (overleaf) near Belle Plaine, Minnesota.

The barn and surrounding cornfields (opposite) near Embden, North Dakota, take a pounding in the state's snowy, sub-zero winters. This nineteenth-century barn (above) near Deadwood was one of South Dakota's first known barns and is believed to be the oldest still standing. Its unusual arched doors and meticulously laid stone walls make it a gem among barns to this day. Dakota farmers, who often lacked much available wood, were ingenious in making use of indigenous materials.

Richard and Lonna Morkert's ten-sided barn (above) outside Sturgis, South Dakota, was built in 1941 as a Hereford bull sale barn. Its vertical pine-pole walls give the structure the appearance of a western stockade. Ventilators like the one atop the barn were sold for many decades out of the Sears catalogue and shipped to farmers and ranchers across America. Lonna Morkert, an avid rider, stables her horse Charger (opposite) inside the barn.

The round barn (top right) in Arcadia, Oklahoma—along legendary U.S. Route 66—was beautifully restored in the 1980s. Round barns deflect the winds of "Tornado Alley," and they can hold a lot of cattle, crowded like wedges of cheese around a central feeder. A farmer near Pampa in the Texas Panhandle turned a simple Quonset (bottom right) into a crude barn. Inside the Child-Kleffner Ranch's big barn in East Helena, Montana, is a classic 1925 Chevrolet truck (opposite).

Visitors come from all over the nation to see
the 1888 Child-Kleffner barn in Montana, with
its seventy windows and twenty-seven-thousand
square feet of floor space. But they get a laugh
from the smallest structure on the ranch—
a martin house (above) fashioned to resemble
the end of the huge barn. Farther west in
Powell County, near the little town of Phosphate,
stands one of the relatively few stylized barns
(right) in the Montana mountains.

Florence and Mike Brennan's striking barn (left), sporting the Lightning Creek Ranch's OK Quarter Circle brand, is one of the most-photographed barns in Oregon's Wallowa County. The barn sits near Prairie Creek against an ancient glacial moraine and the snow-capped peaks of the Wallowa Mountains. La Vonne Denning of Cove, Oregon, commissioned artist Jon Hanley to paint a familiar scene (above) on the family barn as a birthday present for her husband, Johnny—a mule lover.

It took forty-two gallons of paint—and the better part of three summers—
for James Buckles of Joseph, Oregon, to paint his forty-five-foot-high
barn (opposite). It was the final stage of a loving restoration. An old livery
stable (above) is one relic at Columbia State Historic Park in the heart
of California's gold country. It's not hard to guess the favorite sport of the
owner of this barn (overleaf) along Highway 101 near Salinas, California.

The history of America's farming and rural life is told in
dollhouse-scale miniature—one inch equaling one foot—
at the Mini-Americana Barn Museum in South Amana, Iowa.
Beginning with a single model built for his grandchildren,
woodworker and retired farmer Henry Moore created
175 buildings and eight complete scenes. One plantation
house took Moore a year to complete. The animals were
purchased from a South Dakota toy factory and painted
to fit their breed. The museum fills an old, red horse barn.